TEXAS LANGUAGE ARTS
Vocabulary Skills Workbook
Idioms, Adages, Similes, & Metaphors

Skill-Building Practice

for Grade 3, Grade 4, and Grade 5

© 2017 by Test Master Press Texas

All rights reserved. No part of this book may be reproduced or transmitted in any form or by any means, electronic, mechanical, photocopying, recording, or otherwise without prior written permission.

ISBN 978-1975995799

Vocabulary Skills Workbook: Idioms, Adages, Similes, & Metaphors

CONTENTS

Introduction   4

Skill-Building Practice Exercises

   Easy

   Level 1: Exercises 1 to 10   5
   Level 2: Exercises 11 to 20   16
   Level 3: Exercises 21 to 30   27

   Moderate

   Level 4: Exercises 31 to 40   38
   Level 5: Exercises 41 to 50   49
   Level 6: Exercises 51 to 60   60
   Level 7: Exercises 61 to 70   71

   Advanced

   Level 8: Exercises 71 to 80   82
   Level 9: Exercises 81 to 90   93
   Level 10: Exercises 91 to 101   104
   Hyperbole Challenge   116

Answer Key

   Level 1: Exercises 1 to 10   118
   Level 2: Exercises 11 to 20   119
   Level 3: Exercises 21 to 30   120
   Level 4: Exercises 31 to 40   121
   Level 5: Exercises 41 to 50   122
   Level 6: Exercises 51 to 60   123
   Level 7: Exercises 61 to 70   124
   Level 8: Exercises 71 to 80   125
   Level 9: Exercises 81 to 90   126
   Level 10: Exercises 91 to 101   127
   Texas Standards Alignment   128

INTRODUCTION
For Parents, Teachers, and Tutors

Key Terms

This book covers the types of figurative language and sayings summarized in the table below.

	Meaning	Examples
Idiom	a phrase that has a figurative meaning rather than a literal meaning	He is skating on thin ice. She made a song and dance about it.
Simile	the comparison of two things using "like" or "as"	The runner was as fast as lightning. The brothers fight like cats and dogs.
Metaphor	the comparison of two things without the use of "like" or "as"	Life is a rollercoaster. Our mother is a rock.
Hyperbole	the use of exaggeration to emphasize something	I have all the time in the world. I told you to be quiet a million times.
Adage	a well-known saying that expresses a common experience or observation	Bad news travels fast. Opposites attract.

Building Skills

The exercises in this book are divided into 10 levels that progress from easy to advanced. The table below summarizes the general differences between each level.

Level	Difficulty	Features
Levels 1 to 3	Easy	- Grade 2 or 3 vocabulary and reading level - Simpler questions and tasks and more guided tasks - Lower demand on students
Levels 4 to 7	Moderate	- Grade 3 or 4 vocabulary and reading level - Simple to moderate questions and tasks - Higher demand on students and more writing required
Levels 8 to 10	Advanced	- Grade 5 or higher vocabulary and reading level - Moderate to complex questions and tasks - More independent thinking and writing required

Students will first gain the foundation needed to identify, understand, and use figurative language and sayings. Students will apply and build on these skills as they move through the levels. With this leveled approach and focus, students will expand their language skills and advance to a level of ability that reaches and then exceeds their grade level.

Vocabulary Skills Workbook: Idioms, Adages, Similes, & Metaphors

Level 1

Exercises 1 to 10

Difficulty: ★☆☆

Building Your Vocabulary

As you complete the exercises, list any words you have trouble with below. Draw a picture or write down the meaning of each word.

Vocabulary Skills Workbook: Idioms, Adages, Similes, & Metaphors

Exercise 1

Complete the idiom in each sentence. Use the pictures below as clues. Then explain what each sentence means.

1 It was time to hit the *books.*
It was time to study.

2 The test was a piece of _____.
_____

3 The music was not my _____.
_____

4 I had a lot on my _____.
_____

5 I was over the _____ about the win.
_____

Exercise 2

Draw lines to match each sentence with its meaning.

I was hopping mad.   I was happy.

I was down in the dumps.   I was angry.

I was run off my feet.   I was sad.

I was shaking all over.   I was tired.

I was beat.   I was busy.

I was walking on air.   I was scared.

Draw lines to match each phrase with its meaning.

Button your lip.   Calm down.

Get a move on.   Wait.

Hold your horses.   Be quiet.

Shoot for the stars.   Hurry up.

Take it easy.   Aim high.

Exercise 3

Replace the underlined words in each sentence with one of the phrases in the table below.

a handful	slipped up	~~stick around~~
hit the hay	got to run	little by little

1 I would like to <u>stay</u> a bit longer.

   I would like to *stick around* a bit longer.

2 I have <u>a couple</u> of pages left to read.

   I have _____ of pages left to read.

3 I am meeting my friend, so I have <u>to leave</u>.

   I am meeting my friend, so I have _____.

4 I am sorry that I <u>made a mistake</u>.

   I am sorry that I _____.

5 It is getting late, so I might <u>go to bed</u>.

   It is getting late, so I might _____.

6 We made our way up the hill <u>slowly</u>.

   We made our way up the hill _____.

Vocabulary Skills Workbook: Idioms, Adages, Similes, & Metaphors

Exercise 4

List five reasons someone might be in hot water.

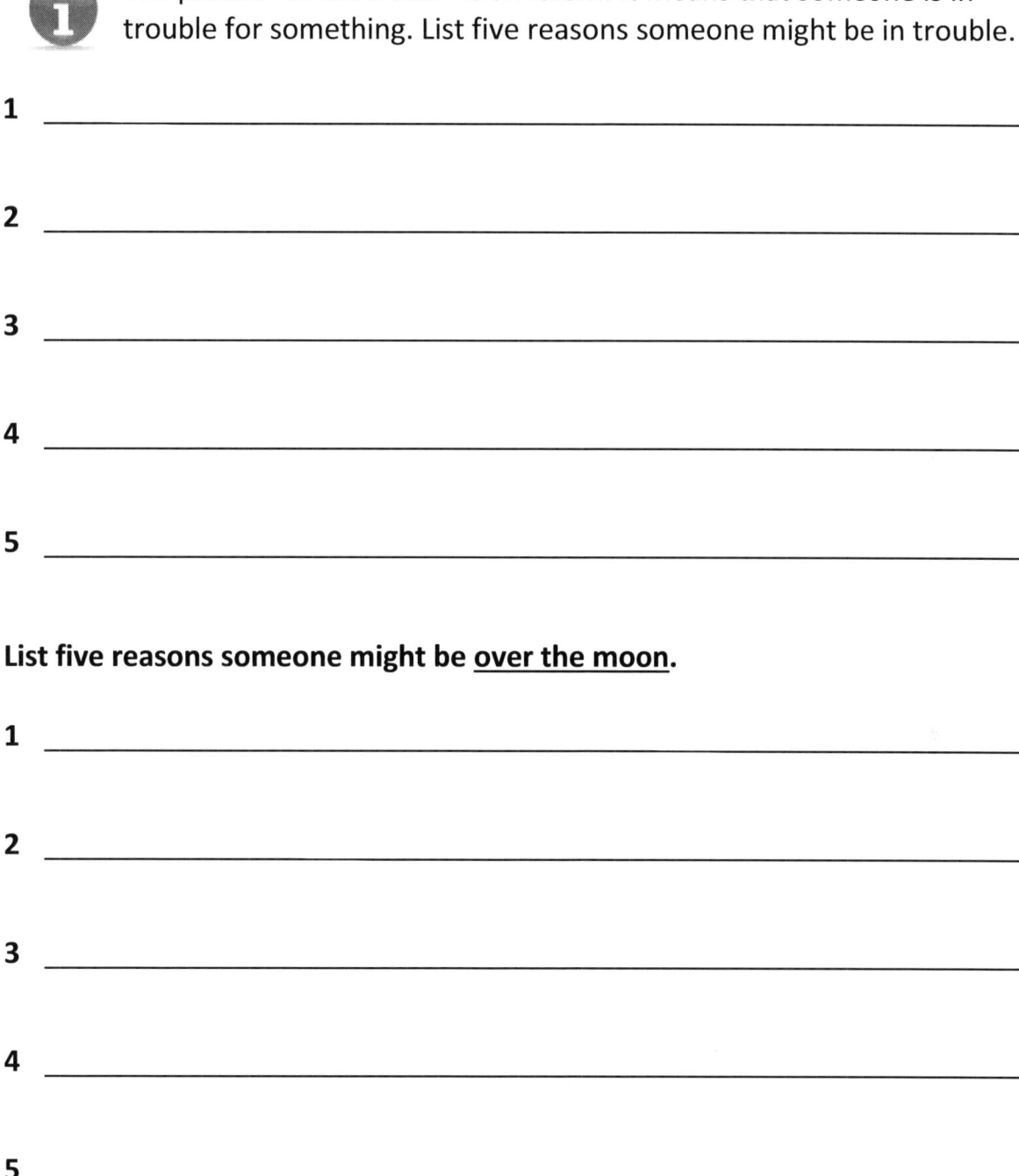

The phrase "in hot water" is an idiom. It means that someone is in trouble for something. List five reasons someone might be in trouble.

1 _____

2 _____

3 _____

4 _____

5 _____

List five reasons someone might be over the moon.

1 _____

2 _____

3 _____

4 _____

5 _____

Vocabulary Skills Workbook: Idioms, Adages, Similes, & Metaphors

Exercise 5

Use the names of the animals shown below to complete each common simile. Write the name of the animal that completes each simile on the blank line.

1 as big as *an elephant*

2 as slow as _____

3 as free as _____

4 as sick as _____

5 as busy as _____

6 as wise as _____

7 as hungry as _____

8 as quiet as _____

Exercise 6

Choose the best answer to each question.

1 Which sentence below includes a simile?
   Ⓐ The room was small.
   Ⓑ The room had green walls.
   Ⓒ The room was neat as a pin.
   Ⓓ The room looked nice.

2 If you "drop someone a line," what are you doing?
   Ⓐ visiting someone
   Ⓑ calling someone
   Ⓒ writing someone a letter
   Ⓓ sending someone a photo

3 Which phrase means "having a problem"?
   Ⓐ in a cherry
   Ⓑ in a pepper
   Ⓒ in a jelly
   Ⓓ in a pickle

4 Which word completes the common phrase below?

   as safe as _____

   Ⓐ boats   Ⓑ buses   Ⓒ houses   Ⓓ farms

5 What does the underlined word in the sentence below mean?

   My little sister always <u>bugs</u> me.

   Ⓐ copies   Ⓑ annoys   Ⓒ watches   Ⓓ follows

Exercise 7

Describe a time in your life when you felt <u>like a fish out of water</u>.

If you feel "like a fish out of water," it means that you feel out of place or like you don't belong. Think of a time when you felt like that. Describe when you felt like that and why you felt like that.

_____

_____

_____

_____

_____

Describe a time in your life when you <u>chickened out</u> of doing something.

Start by deciding what the underlined phrase means.

_____

_____

_____

_____

_____

Vocabulary Skills Workbook: Idioms, Adages, Similes, & Metaphors

Exercise 8

Choose the word that completes each sentence. Write the correct word on the line.

1 lemon   orange   apple   banana

   Joe's new car broke down. He bought a _____.

2 blue   yellow   green   red

   Sonia is good at gardening. She has a _____ thumb.

3 dog   fish   rabbit   cat

   Perry did not know what to say. The _____ had his tongue.

4 paper   wool   glass   wood

   Kareem tricked me. He pulled the _____ over my eyes.

5 rain   snow   wind   sun

   Yumi ran fast. She ran like the _____.

6 bag   cart   drawer   pantry

   We knew we would win. We had the win in the _____.

Exercise 9

Each saying gives a piece of advice or a lesson. Explain what the lesson is in your own words.

1. There's no use crying over spilled milk.

   Don't be upset over something that has happened. It cannot be changed, so don't worry about it.

2. You shouldn't judge a book by its cover.

   _____

   _____

3. You can't teach an old dog new tricks.

   _____

   _____

4. There is no such thing as a free lunch.

   _____

   _____

5. Slow and steady wins the race.

   _____

   _____

Exercise 10

Complete each common saying by writing the missing word on the line. Use each word listed below once.

    fire   roses   cake   trees   horse

    apple   eggs   worm   grass   chickens

1 Money doesn't grow on _____.

2 Don't put all your _____ in one basket.

3 You can't have your _____ and eat it too.

4 The early bird gets the _____.

5 Don't count your _____ until they're hatched.

6 You should stop to smell the _____.

7 An _____ a day keeps the doctor away.

8 Where there is smoke, there is _____.

9 The _____ is always greener on the other side.

10 Don't put the cart before the _____.

Level 2

Exercises 11 to 20

Difficulty: ★☆☆

Building Your Vocabulary

As you complete the exercises, list any words you have trouble with below. Draw a picture or write down the meaning of each word.

Exercise 11

Complete the idiom in each sentence. Use the pictures below as clues. Then use each idiom in a sentence.

1 on *cloud* nine
   I felt like I was on cloud nine when I won.

2 throw in the _____

   _____

3 hit the _____

   _____

4 ring a _____

   _____

5 spill the _____

   _____

Exercise 12

Each sentence has an idiom underlined. Write the meaning of the idiom on the blank line.

 Remember that an idiom has a special meaning other than the one you can guess from the meaning of each individual word.

1 I passed the math test <u>with flying colors</u>. *easily*

2 Jasmine was feeling <u>under the weather</u>. _____

3 The park is <u>a stone's throw away</u>. _____

4 The race was <u>neck and neck</u>. _____

5 They left at nine o'clock <u>on the dot</u>. _____

6 I had to <u>keep an eye on</u> my brother. _____

7 The toys are selling <u>like hotcakes</u>. _____

8 I was finally starting to <u>get the picture</u>. _____

9 We are late, so we should <u>step on the gas</u>. _____

10 I asked Donna if she could <u>give me a hand</u>. _____

Exercise 13

Replace the underlined words in each sentence with one of the phrases in the table below.

get a move on	by heart	~~right away~~
cut it out	hit it off	around the clock

1 Your food will be cold if you don't come to dinner <u>very soon</u>.

   Your food will be cold if you don't come to dinner *right away*.

2 Dad was tired of our fighting, and told us to <u>stop it</u>.

   Dad was tired of our fighting, and told us to _____.

3 When Joan and I met, we <u>liked each other</u> right away.

   When Joan and I met, we _____ right away.

4 If we are going to make the train, we need to <u>hurry up</u>.

   If we are going to make the train, we need to _____.

5 The grocery store is open <u>all the time</u>.

   The grocery store is open _____.

6 I have sung the song so many times that I know it <u>really well</u>.

   I have sung the song so many times that I know it _____.

Exercise 14

List five reasons someone might <u>go red in the face</u>.

> The phrase "go red in the face" is an idiom. It means that someone is embarrassed. List five reasons someone might feel embarrassed.

1 _____

2 _____

3 _____

4 _____

5 _____

List five items that might cost <u>an arm and a leg</u>.

1 _____

2 _____

3 _____

4 _____

5 _____

Exercise 15

Use the names of the objects shown below to complete each common simile. Write the name of the object that completes each simile on the blank line.

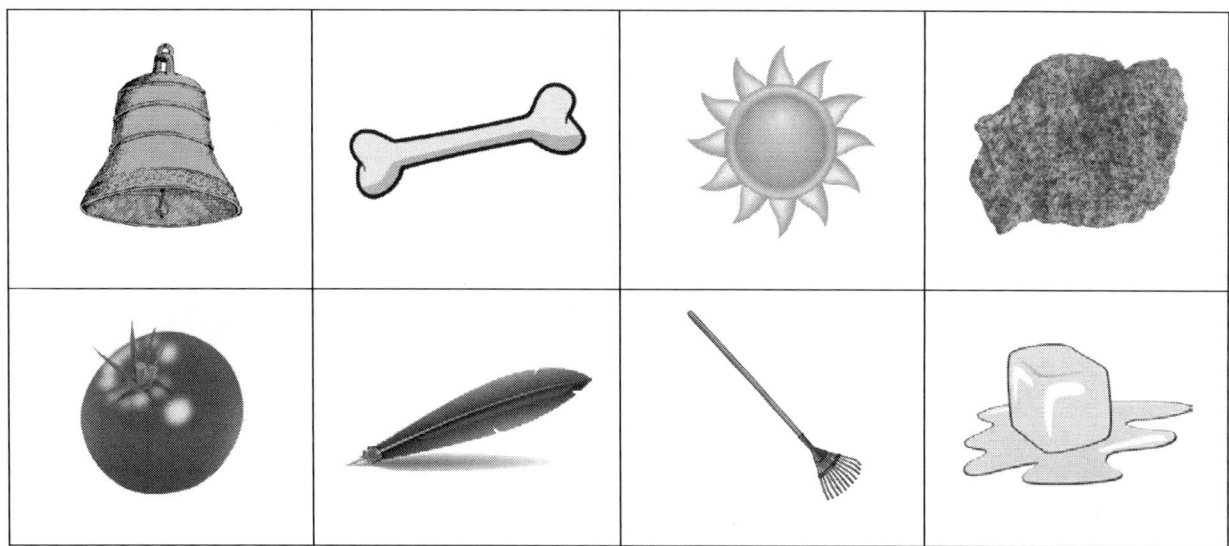

1 as thin as _____

2 as solid as _____

3 as cold as _____

4 as light as _____

5 as dry as _____

6 as bright as _____

7 as clear as _____

8 as red as _____

Exercise 16

Choose the best answer to each question.

1. What is the message of the saying below mainly about?

    Count your blessings.

    Ⓐ being careful   Ⓒ being helpful
    Ⓑ being thankful   Ⓓ being hopeful

2. If something is "like watching paint dry," it is
    Ⓐ boring   Ⓒ strange
    Ⓑ exciting   Ⓓ normal

3. Which phrase means "a bad person"?
    Ⓐ a rotten apple   Ⓒ a rotten orange
    Ⓑ a rotten pear   Ⓓ a rotten peach

4. Which word completes the phrase that means "to tell how you really feel"?

    to give someone a piece of your _____

    Ⓐ cake   Ⓑ pizza   Ⓒ mind   Ⓓ clothing

5. What does the underlined phrase in the sentence below mean?

    The book was a real page-turner.

    Ⓐ very long   Ⓑ very short   Ⓒ very good   Ⓓ very bad

Exercise 17

Describe a time in your life when you felt like you were <u>on cloud nine</u>.

If you feel like you are "on cloud nine," it means that you feel very happy. Think of a time when you felt like that. Describe when you felt like that and why you felt like that.

_____

_____

_____

_____

_____

_____

Describe a time when you <u>pulled someone's leg</u>.

Start by deciding what the underlined phrase means.

_____

_____

_____

_____

_____

Exercise 18

Choose the word that best completes each sentence. Write the correct word on the line.

1 red-handed   blue-handed   green-handed   pink-handed

   Michael was caught stealing. He was caught _____.

2 bull   tiger   frog   duck

   Riku was an easy target. He was a sitting _____.

3 dog   fish   bird   cat

   I had a short sleep. I had a _____ nap.

4 bee   fly   moth   beetle

   Mandy is very nice. She wouldn't hurt a _____.

5 branch   seed   leaf   flower

   Omar has changed. He has turned over a new _____.

6 cold   salty   clear   deep

   Emily has a serious problem. She is in _____ water.

Exercise 19

Each saying offers a lesson. Explain what the lesson is in your own words. Then give an example of a time you used, or could have used, the lesson.

1. Every cloud has a silver lining.

   Lesson: *Every bad thing has something good about it.*
   Example: *I was sick last week. The good thing about it was I got to stay home and watch movies.*

2. It's better to be safe than sorry.

   Lesson: _____

   _____

   Example: _____

   _____

   _____

3. Many hands make light work.

   Lesson: _____

   _____

   Example: _____

   _____

   _____

Exercise 20

Complete each common saying by writing the missing word on the line. Use each word listed below once.

| cat | glass | hay | dog | leopard |
| baby | horse | bird | fire | forest |

1 If you play with _____, you will get burned.

2 They can't see the _____ for the trees.

3 Don't throw the _____ out with the bathwater.

4 Curiosity killed the _____.

5 A _____ in the hand is worth two in the bush.

6 Every _____ has his day.

7 Don't look a gift _____ in the mouth.

8 People who live in _____ houses shouldn't throw stones.

9 Make _____ while the sun shines.

10 A _____ cannot change its spots.

Vocabulary Skills Workbook: Idioms, Adages, Similes, & Metaphors

Level 3

Exercises 21 to 30

Difficulty: ★☆☆

Building Your Vocabulary

As you complete the exercises, list any words you have trouble with below. Draw a picture or write down the meaning of each word.

Vocabulary Skills Workbook: Idioms, Adages, Similes, & Metaphors

Exercise 21

Complete the idiom in each sentence. Use the pictures below as clues. Then use each idiom in a sentence.

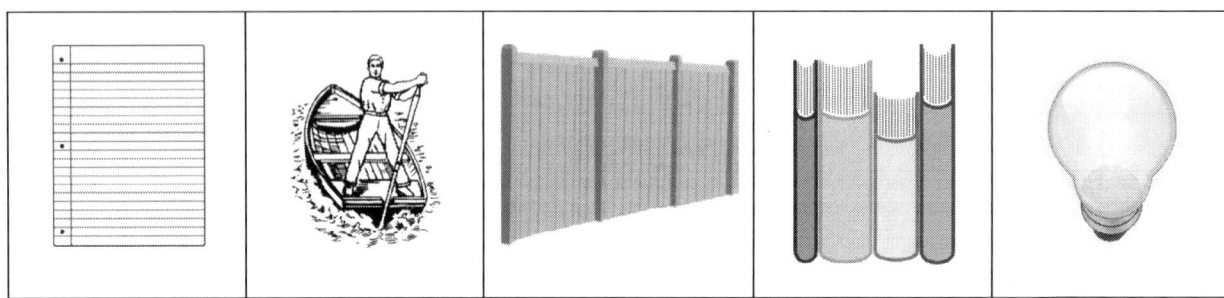

1 in my good _____

2 on the _____

3 on the same _____

4 see the _____

5 rock the _____

Exercise 22

Each sentence has an idiom underlined. Write the meaning of the idiom on the blank line.

 You can use the way the idiom is used in the sentence to help you work out its meaning.

1 The jokes that Matt told had us <u>in stitches</u>.   *laughing a lot*

2 The shoes at the sale were <u>a steal</u>.   _____

3 When the speaker talked, everyone was <u>all ears</u>.   _____

4 The project failed because we <u>cut corners</u>.   _____

5 I <u>gave my word</u> that I would not let her down.   _____

6 The test I took yesterday was <u>child's play</u>.   _____

7 We had a great plan <u>right from the word go</u>.   _____

8 They are twins, but they are <u>like chalk and cheese</u>.   _____

9 It was a long race, and I <u>ran out of steam</u> halfway.   _____

10 The thought of seeing a bear had me <u>shaking in my boots</u>.   _____

Exercise 23

Replace the underlined words in each sentence with one of the phrases in the table below.

~~like clockwork~~	face to face	in a flash
on a roll	up and running	come in handy

1. After years of working together, our science club runs <u>very smoothly</u>.

   After years of working together, our science club runs *like clockwork*.

2. I know Cleo would be here <u>quickly</u> if I needed her.

   I know Cleo would be here _____ if I needed her.

3. It is good to see that the old factory is <u>working</u> again.

   It is good to see that the old factory is _____ again.

4. We had sent letters for years, but had never met <u>in person</u>.

   We had sent letters for years, but had never met _____.

5. The sewing kit in my bag might <u>be useful</u> one day.

   The sewing kit in my bag might _____ one day.

6. Our team was <u>doing very well</u> and had not lost a game.

   Our team was _____ and had not lost a game.

Exercise 24

List five reasons you might feel <u>down in the dumps</u>.

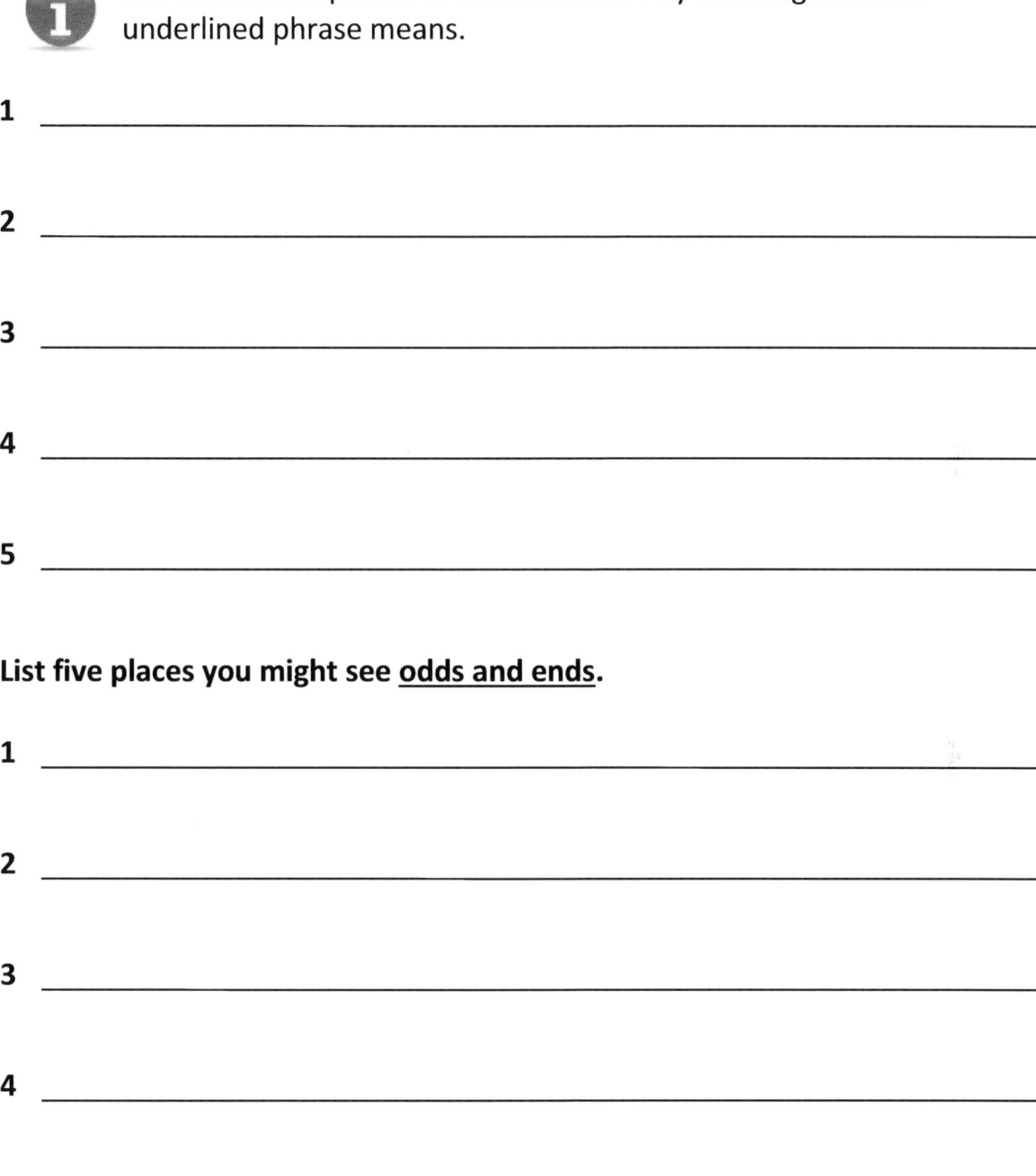 The underlined phrase is an idiom. Start by deciding what the underlined phrase means.

1 _____

2 _____

3 _____

4 _____

5 _____

List five places you might see <u>odds and ends</u>.

1 _____

2 _____

3 _____

4 _____

5 _____

Vocabulary Skills Workbook: Idioms, Adages, Similes, & Metaphors

Exercise 25

Use the names of the animals shown below to complete each common simile. Write the name of the animal that completes each simile on the blank line.

1 as brave as _____

2 as sly as _____

3 as proud as _____

4 as strong as _____

5 as busy as _____

6 as gentle as _____

7 as hungry as _____

8 as slippery as _____

Exercise 26

Choose the best answer to each question.

1. Which sentence below includes an idiom?
   - Ⓐ Joy wants to be a painter one day.
   - Ⓑ Joy takes art classes every week.
   - Ⓒ Joy is on the right track.
   - Ⓓ Joy sold her first painting last month.

2. If you are told to "use your loaf," what are you being told to do?
   - Ⓐ eat
   - Ⓑ think
   - Ⓒ drink
   - Ⓓ move

3. Which word is used to describe something that is very easy?
   - Ⓐ gust
   - Ⓑ puff
   - Ⓒ blast
   - Ⓓ breeze

4. Which word completes the common saying below?

    Time _____ when you are having fun.

   - Ⓐ skips
   - Ⓑ bounces
   - Ⓒ flies
   - Ⓓ walks

5. Which word completes the phrase that means "to take a chance"?

    to stick your _____ out

   - Ⓐ neck
   - Ⓑ hand
   - Ⓒ tongue
   - Ⓓ foot

Exercise 27

Describe a time in your life when you <u>gave something your all</u>.

Start by deciding what the underlined phrase means.

_____
_____
_____
_____

Describe a time in your life when you were given <u>a pat on the back</u>.

Describe what you did and why you were given a pat on the back.

_____
_____
_____
_____

Exercise 28

Choose the word that best completes each sentence. Write the correct word on the line.

1 deep   dark   black   red

They wouldn't tell us anything. They kept us in the _____.

2 barn   bear   block   bush

She wouldn't get to the point. She was beating around the _____.

3 hat   glove   shoe   coat

I would leave any time. I would leave at the drop of a _____.

4 wire   nail   glue   rope

The game was very close. It came down to the _____.

5 bowls   forks   knives   plates

The boys are being very mean to each other. The _____ are out.

6 arm   hair   leg   ear

He is trying to trick me. He is pulling my _____.

Exercise 29

Each saying offers a lesson. Explain what the lesson is in your own words. Then give an example of a time you used, or could have used, the lesson.

1. Rome was not built in a day.

   Lesson: *It takes time to get things done.*
   Example: *I got upset when I was not good at painting. I learned it takes time to get good at it.*

2. You should always look on the bright side.

   Lesson: _____

   _____

   Example: _____

   _____

   _____

3. You can't have your cake and eat it too.

   Lesson: _____

   _____

   Example: _____

   _____

   _____

Exercise 30

Complete each common saying by writing the missing word on the line. Use each word listed below once.

    golden   never   shy   free   present

    sorry   broken   right   hot   burned

1 Once bitten, twice _____.

2 If you play with fire, you will get _____.

3 It's better to be safe than _____.

4 The best things in life are _____.

5 Silence is _____.

6 Two wrongs don't make a _____.

7 It's better late than _____.

8 You should strike while the iron is _____.

9 There is no time like the _____.

10 Even a _____ watch is right twice a day.

Vocabulary Skills Workbook: Idioms, Adages, Similes, & Metaphors

Level 4

Exercises 31 to 40

Difficulty: ★★☆

Building Your Vocabulary

As you complete the exercises, list any words you have trouble with below. Draw a picture or write down the meaning of each word.

Exercise 31

Complete the idiom in each sentence. Use the pictures below as clues. Then use each idiom in a sentence.

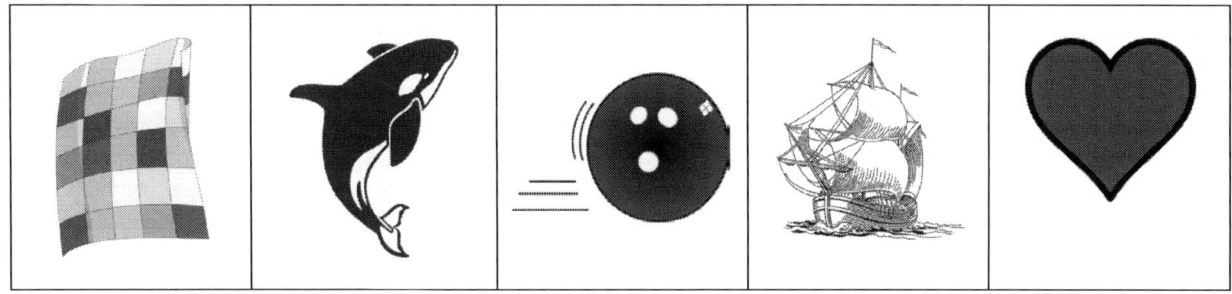

1 on a _____

   _____

2 smooth _____

   _____

3 change of _____

   _____

4 a _____ of a time

   _____

5 a wet _____

   _____

Exercise 32

Underline the idiom in each sentence. Then write the meaning of the idiom on the blank line.

1. Even though the computer was on sale, it still <u>cost an arm and a leg</u>.

    cost a lot of money

2. I felt bad about scratching my sister's bike, so I finally came clean about it.

    _____

3. I like reading mystery stories, so the book was right up my alley.

    _____

4. Claudia is one of my favorite people because she is always a barrel of laughs.

    _____

5. I did not know the answer to the question, so I took a shot in the dark.

    _____

6. We tried to solve the puzzle, but nobody could make head or tail of it.

    _____

Exercise 33

Replace the underlined words in each sentence with one of the phrases in the table below.

out of the blue	for a song	keep a straight face
have a soft spot for	gave a big hand	steer clear of

1. I always <u>stay away from</u> that street because of the big dog.

   I always _____ that street because of the big dog.

2. The people in the crowd <u>clapped loudly</u> for the band.

   The people in the crowd _____ for the band.

3. I <u>really like</u> kittens and other cute animals.

   I _____ kittens and other cute animals.

4. I tried to <u>stop myself from laughing</u>, but I could not help but giggle.

   I tried to _____, but I could not help but giggle.

5. I got soaked when the shower came <u>without warning</u>.

   I got soaked when the shower came _____.

6. The sale was really good. I got this bag <u>very cheaply</u>.

   The sale was really good. I got this bag _____.

Vocabulary Skills Workbook: Idioms, Adages, Similes, & Metaphors

Exercise 34

List five foods you might <u>pig out on</u>.

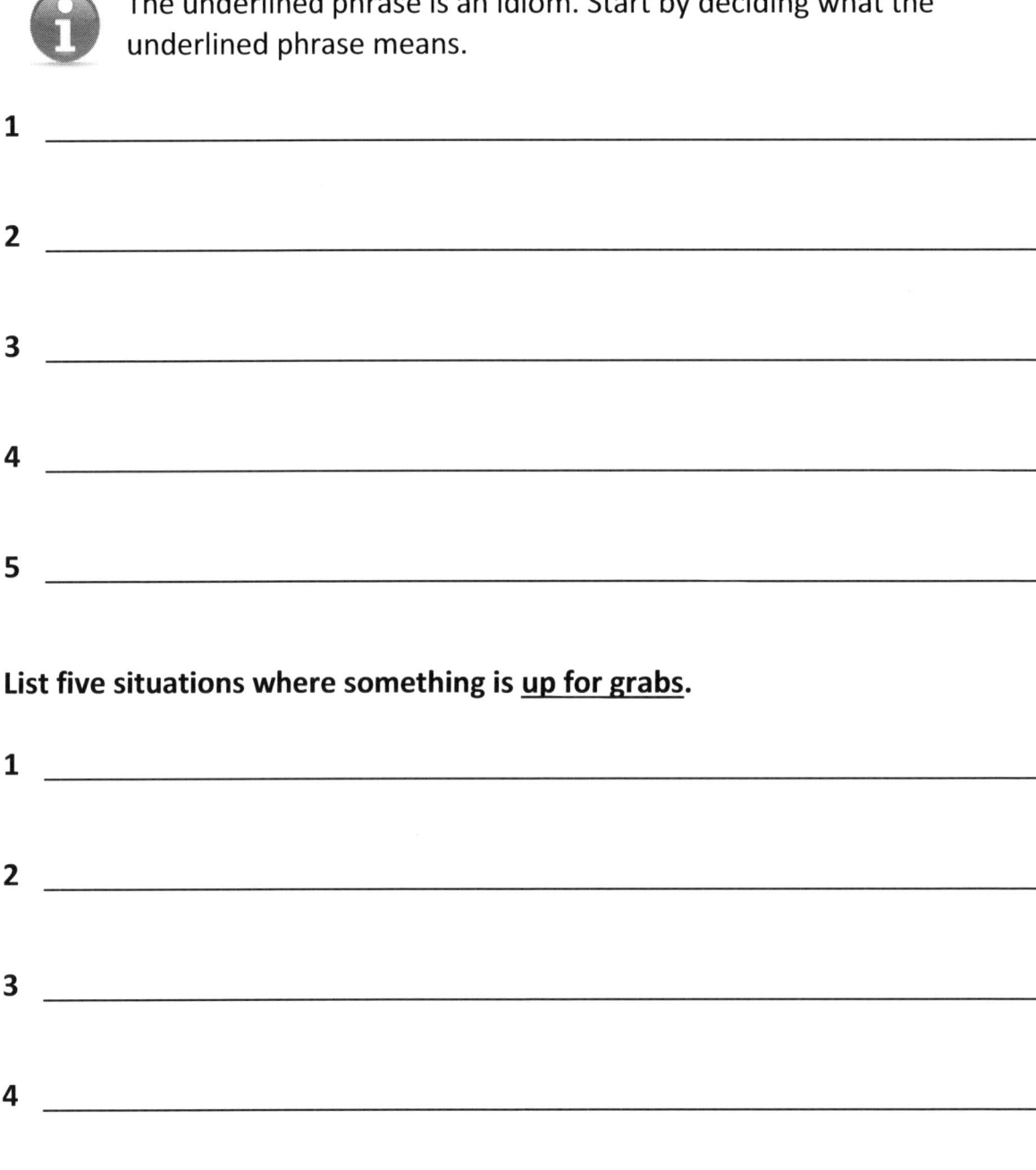 The underlined phrase is an idiom. Start by deciding what the underlined phrase means.

1 _____

2 _____

3 _____

4 _____

5 _____

List five situations where something is <u>up for grabs</u>.

1 _____

2 _____

3 _____

4 _____

5 _____

Vocabulary Skills Workbook: Idioms, Adages, Similes, & Metaphors

Exercise 35

Use the names of the objects shown below to complete each common simile. Write the name of the object that completes each simile on the blank line. Then use the simile in a sentence.

1 as pretty as a _____

   _____

2 as warm as _____

   _____

3 as easy as _____

   _____

4 as fresh as a _____

   _____

43

Vocabulary Skills Workbook: Idioms, Adages, Similes, & Metaphors

Exercise 36

Choose the best answer to each question.

1. What is the main message of the saying below about?

    You scratch my back and I'll scratch yours.

    Ⓐ taking chances   Ⓒ helping each other
    Ⓑ having goals   Ⓓ being careful

2. If two people are "at odds with each other," what are they doing?
    Ⓐ working together   Ⓒ becoming friends
    Ⓑ disagreeing   Ⓓ celebrating

3. Which phrase means "to blame someone else"?
    Ⓐ to pass the buck   Ⓒ to pass the time
    Ⓑ to pass the hat   Ⓓ to pass the torch

4. Which word best completes the sentence below?

    Ryan tried to break the _____ by telling a joke.

    Ⓐ bank   Ⓑ promise   Ⓒ ice   Ⓓ record

5. Which word completes the phrase that means "to talk highly of yourself"?

    to blow your own _____

    Ⓐ tuba   Ⓑ flute   Ⓒ trumpet   Ⓓ saxophone

Exercise 37

Describe a time when you tried something that was <u>not your cup of tea</u>.

Start by deciding what the underlined phrase means.

_____
_____
_____
_____
_____

Describe a time in your life when you had to <u>come clean about something</u>.

Describe what you came clean about and what happened.

_____
_____
_____
_____
_____

Exercise 38

Each sentence uses an idiom to describe a person. Finish each paragraph by giving a detail to support the first sentence.

 Start by working out what the idiom is telling you about the person.

1 Marvin has the gift of the gab. *He often talks to people he meets while waiting for the bus.*

2 Joanne is a night owl. _____

3 Alberto is two-faced. _____

4 Rosita is a busybody. _____

5 Todd is a daredevil. _____

6 Wesley is a whiz kid. _____

Exercise 39

Each saying offers a lesson. Explain what the lesson is in your own words. Then give an example of a time you used, or could have used, the lesson.

1 Don't put all your eggs in one basket.

   Lesson: _____

   _____

   Example: _____

   _____

   _____

   _____

2 There are two sides to every story.

   Lesson: _____

   _____

   Example: _____

   _____

   _____

   _____

Exercise 40

A proverb is a common saying that states a truth. For each proverb, write a paragraph or two explaining whether or not you agree. Explain why you feel that way.

1   Practice makes perfect.

2   Honesty is the best policy.

Level 5

Exercises 41 to 50

Difficulty: ★★☆

Building Your Vocabulary

As you complete the exercises, list any words you have trouble with below. Draw a picture or write down the meaning of each word.

Exercise 41

Complete the idiom in each sentence with the correct set of words. Then explain the meaning of each sentence in your own words.

the bed	~~blue moon~~	cats and dogs
your court	new leaf	eye to eye

1. It happens once in a *blue moon*.
   It happens very rarely.

2. He got up on the wrong side of _____.

   _____

3. They did not see _____.

   _____

4. She turned over a _____.

   _____

5. It was raining _____.

   _____

6. The ball is in _____.

   _____

Exercise 42

Underline the idiom in each sentence. Then write the meaning of the idiom on the blank line.

1. It was still raining, so I was in two minds about going to the beach.

   _____

2. The two-year-old child flies off the handle every time his mother goes out.

   _____

3. The time for the dance was not set in stone.

   _____

4. We had to start from scratch because the toy plane we made did not fly at all.

   _____

5. I could not decide what the best choice was, so I decided to sleep on it.

   _____

6. It is unfair to a hard worker if all team members do not pull their weight.

   _____

Exercise 43

Complete each sentence.

 Start by thinking about what the idiom at the start of each sentence means. Then think of a way to finish the sentence that makes sense.

1 I lost my cool when _____

_____

2 I was in a jam because _____

_____

3 I was thrilled to bits when _____

_____

4 I put my foot in it when _____

_____

5 I kept my fingers crossed because _____

_____

6 I was at the end of my rope because _____

_____

Exercise 44

List five items that might be described as <u>state of the art</u>.

 The underlined phrase is an idiom. Start by deciding what the underlined phrase means.

1 _____

2 _____

3 _____

4 _____

5 _____

List five places where there is <u>no room to swing a cat</u>.

1 _____

2 _____

3 _____

4 _____

5 _____

Exercise 45

Complete each common simile. Use the pictures below as clues. Write the word that completes each simile on the blank line. Then use the simile in a sentence.

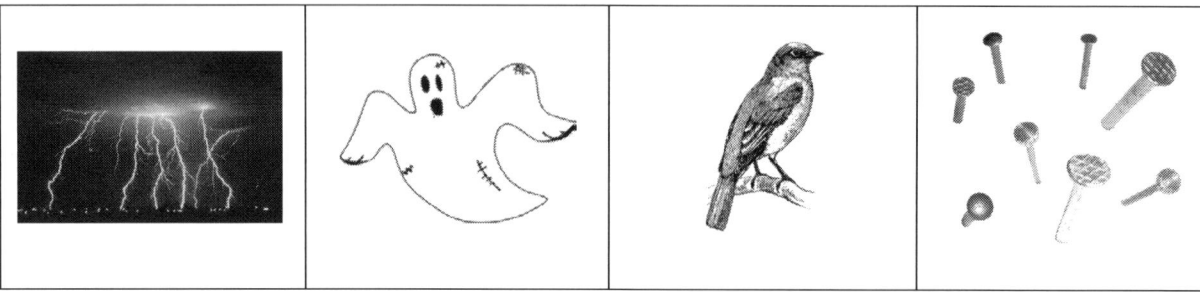

1 as tough as _____

   _____

2 sing like a _____

   _____

3 as white as a _____

   _____

4 as fast as _____

   _____

Exercise 46

Choose the best answer to each question.

1. What is the main message of the saying below about?

    Look before you leap.

    Ⓐ being determined   Ⓒ being outgoing
    Ⓑ being thoughtful   Ⓓ being cautious

2. Which phrase can be used to describe people who are very similar?

    Ⓐ like chalk and cheese   Ⓒ peas in a pod
    Ⓑ like night and day   Ⓓ poles apart

3. Which phrase means "to hurry up"?

    Ⓐ pick up the tab   Ⓒ pick up the pieces
    Ⓑ pick up the pace   Ⓓ pick up the slack

4. Which word best completes the sentence below?

    The problem with the poster was as plain as _____.

    Ⓐ dirt   Ⓑ snow   Ⓒ night   Ⓓ day

5. Which word completes the phrase that means "not decided"?

    the _____ is still out

    Ⓐ jury   Ⓑ dog   Ⓒ fire   Ⓓ trash

Exercise 47

Describe a time when you felt like you were in over your head.

Start by deciding what the underlined phrase means.

_____

_____

_____

_____

_____

Describe a time in your life when you decided to speak your mind.

Describe what you decided to speak your mind about and why.

_____

_____

_____

_____

_____

Vocabulary Skills Workbook: Idioms, Adages, Similes, & Metaphors

Exercise 48

Write two or three lines of dialogue that includes the given sentence. Make sure your use of the sentence makes sense.

1 "No sweat!"

   "Could you help me with this homework?"
   "No sweat!"
   "Thank you so much."

2 "You can say that again."

   _____

   _____

   _____

3 "Fat chance!"

   _____

   _____

   _____

4 "It's about time."

   _____

   _____

   _____

Exercise 49

Each saying offers a lesson. Explain what the lesson is in your own words. Then give an example of a time you used, or could have used, the lesson.

1 Laughter is the best medicine.

Lesson: _____

_____

Example: _____

_____

_____

_____

2 A trouble shared is a trouble halved.

Lesson: _____

_____

Example: _____

_____

_____

_____

Exercise 50

For each proverb, write a paragraph or two describing a situation in your life that showed that the saying is true.

 For the first question, you could describe a time where you worked with someone to get something done.

1 Two heads are better than one.

_____

_____

_____

_____

_____

2 The best things in life are free.

_____

_____

_____

_____

_____

Level 6

Exercises 51 to 60

Difficulty:

Building Your Vocabulary

As you complete the exercises, list any words you have trouble with below. Draw a picture or write down the meaning of each word.

Exercise 51

Complete the idiom in each sentence with the correct set of words. Then explain the meaning of each sentence in your own words.

the kitchen sink	~~the crack of dawn~~	the same boat
the world	the wrong tree	the bag

1 We got up at *the crack of dawn*.
   We got up very early.

2 I let the cat out of _____.

   _____

3 He packed everything but _____.

   _____

4 She was barking up _____.

   _____

5 We were all in _____.

   _____

6 I felt on top of _____.

   _____

Exercise 52

Underline the idiom in each sentence. Then write the meaning of the idiom on the blank line.

 You can use the context as a clue to the meaning of the idiom.

1 Henry is known for having deep pockets, so we hope he will donate a lot.

   _____

2 Razi dragged her feet for so long that her friends finally left without her.

   _____

3 I felt on edge all day as I waited for the call to tell me whether I had won.

   _____

4 Miss Kimura likes to keep her students on their toes by giving surprise tests.

   _____

5 The students were on the same page about what movie they wanted to see.

   _____

6 I asked Kara to meet me because I had a bone to pick with her.

   _____

Exercise 53

Write the meaning of each idiom on the line. Then use the idiom in a sentence.

 Remember to use the special meaning of each phrase, and not the literal meaning.

1 had a brainwave   *had a good idea*

   Oliver invented a new phone after he had a brainwave.

2 in a heartbeat   _____

   _____

3 bit my head off   _____

   _____

4 on the money   _____

   _____

5 in the ballpark   _____

   _____

6 lost his temper   _____

   _____

Vocabulary Skills Workbook: Idioms, Adages, Similes, & Metaphors

Exercise 54

List five things someone might do to <u>drive you up the wall</u>.

> Start by deciding what the underlined phrase means.

1 _____

2 _____

3 _____

4 _____

5 _____

Choose one of the things you listed above. Write a paragraph describing a situation where someone <u>drove you up the wall</u>. The situation could be real or made up. Explain what the person did and how you felt.

_____

_____

_____

_____

_____

Vocabulary Skills Workbook: Idioms, Adages, Similes, & Metaphors

Exercise 55

Complete each common simile. Use the pictures below as clues. Write the word that completes each simile on the blank line. Then use the simile in a sentence.

  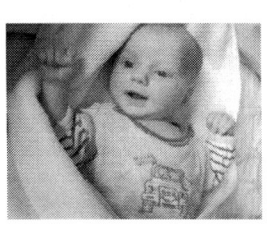 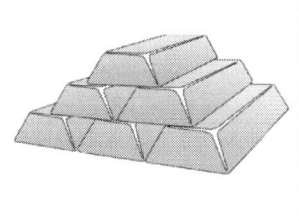

1 sleep like a _____

_____

2 as old as the _____

_____

3 as good as _____

_____

4 as straight as an _____

_____

Exercise 56

Choose the best answer to each question.

1. What does the underlined phrase in the sentence below mean?

    Rodney <u>hit the roof</u> when he saw that his car was missing.

    Ⓐ was surprised   Ⓒ was puzzled
    Ⓑ became angry   Ⓓ became worried

2. If you are giving someone "a wide berth," what are you doing?

    Ⓐ avoiding someone   Ⓒ helping someone
    Ⓑ copying someone   Ⓓ teasing someone

3. Which phrase is commonly used to describe someone as well-dressed?

    Ⓐ You look swift.   Ⓒ You look sharp.
    Ⓑ You look strong.   Ⓓ You look stern.

4. Which word completes the phrase that means "to be too focused on dreams and wishes"?

    to have your head in the _____

    Ⓐ sand   Ⓑ clouds   Ⓒ bucket   Ⓓ rocks

5. What does the underlined word in the sentence below mean?

    The price of the car is <u>steep</u>.

    Ⓐ cheap   Ⓑ costly   Ⓒ increasing   Ⓓ decreasing

Exercise 57

Describe a time when you and someone else <u>got off on the wrong foot</u>.

> Start by deciding what the underlined phrase means.

_____

_____

_____

_____

_____

Describe a time when you <u>had to put your foot down</u> about something.

> Describe what you put your foot down about and why.

_____

_____

_____

_____

_____

Exercise 58

Idioms and phrases can make stories more interesting or more exciting. Write a paragraph or two that includes any two of the phrases listed.

1 a narrow escape   now or never   dark as night

_____

_____

_____

_____

2 middle of nowhere   ran out of steam   on pins and needles

_____

_____

_____

_____

Vocabulary Skills Workbook: Idioms, Adages, Similes, & Metaphors

Exercise 59

Each saying offers a lesson. Explain what the lesson is in your own words. Then give an example of a time you used, or could have used, the lesson.

1 Curiosity killed the cat.

   Lesson: _____

   _____

   Example: _____

   _____

   _____

   _____

2 One person's trash is another person's treasure.

   Lesson: _____

   _____

   Example: _____

   _____

   _____

   _____

Exercise 60

A proverb is a common saying that states a truth. For each proverb, write a paragraph or two explaining whether or not you agree. Explain why you feel that way.

1 Good things come to those who wait.

_____

_____

_____

_____

_____

2 A leopard does not change its spots.

_____

_____

_____

_____

_____

Level 7

Exercises 61 to 70

Difficulty:

Building Your Vocabulary

As you complete the exercises, list any words you have trouble with below. Draw a picture or write down the meaning of each word.

Exercise 61

Complete the idiom in each sentence with the correct animal.

bull	bear	whale
sheep	goat	hog
ducks	rat	horses

1 I could not believe that Mark would _____ on his friends.

2 Everyone had a _____ of a time at the party.

3 Kevin often feels like the black _____ of his family.

4 Steve is like a _____ with a sore head when he is tired.

5 The road _____ was upsetting a lot of other drivers.

6 The way Tessa lies all the time really gets my _____.

7 I finally decided to take the _____ by the horns and do it myself.

8 The party was so great that wild _____ could not have dragged me away.

9 Before the project started, Erin made sure she had all her _____ in a row.

Exercise 62

Underline the idiom in each sentence. Then write the meaning of the idiom on the blank line.

1. The two grandfathers often sit on the porch chewing the fat.

   _____

2. I was kicking myself for missing the winning shot.

   _____

3. My father said that going on a plane by myself was out of the question.

   _____

4. Everything was going very well at first, but then we hit a snag.

   _____

5. The first time I gave a speech, I was a bundle of nerves the whole day before.

   _____

6. The plan to go fishing went out the window when it started raining.

   _____

Vocabulary Skills Workbook: Idioms, Adages, Similes, & Metaphors

Exercise 63

Replace the underlined words in each sentence with one of the phrases in the table below. Then explain what each sentence means.

like wildfire	hit the road	a walk in the park
had a blast	on the blink	iron out

1 The news spread *like wildfire*.

   The news spread quickly.

2 The fridge is _____.

   _____

3 We had to _____ some problems.

   _____

4 The test was _____.

   _____

5 We _____ at eight o'clock.

   _____

6 Everyone _____ at the party.

   _____

Exercise 64

List five situations where someone could be <u>on the fence</u> about something.

1 _____

2 _____

3 _____

4 _____

5 _____

Choose one of the situations you listed above. Write a paragraph describing a time where someone is <u>on the fence</u>. It could be real or made up. Explain what the person is on the fence about and why the person feels that way.

_____

_____

_____

_____

_____

_____

Exercise 65

Each sentence below uses a metaphor to describe someone. Explain the meaning of each metaphor.

1. Chandra has the heart of a lion.

   _____

2. Sonny is an early bird.

   _____

3. Natasha is just being a baby about it.

   _____

4. Felipe has a heart of gold.

   _____

5. Patrick is always being a clown.

   _____

6. Erica is the shining star on our softball team.

   _____

Vocabulary Skills Workbook: Idioms, Adages, Similes, & Metaphors

Exercise 66

Choose the best answer to each question.

1. Which sentence below is an exaggeration?
   - Ⓐ I have several things to do.
   - Ⓑ I have a list of things to do.
   - Ⓒ I have two or three things to do.
   - Ⓓ I have a million things to do.

2. If someone has "slipped up," what has the person done?
   - Ⓐ told a lie
   - Ⓑ fallen over
   - Ⓒ made a mistake
   - Ⓓ spent a lot

3. Which phrase means "to give in to what someone wants"?
   - Ⓐ cave in
   - Ⓑ fall in
   - Ⓒ take in
   - Ⓓ stop in

4. What does the underlined word in the sentence mean?

   Our friendship has been very <u>rocky</u> lately.

   - Ⓐ strong
   - Ⓑ exciting
   - Ⓒ strange
   - Ⓓ difficult

5. Which word completes the phrase that means "at the last minute"?

   at the _____ hour

   - Ⓐ tenth
   - Ⓑ eleventh
   - Ⓒ twelfth
   - Ⓓ thirteenth

Vocabulary Skills Workbook: Idioms, Adages, Similes, & Metaphors

Exercise 67

Describe a time when you <u>bent over backwards</u> for someone.

Describe who you bent over backwards for and what you did.

_____

_____

_____

_____

_____

Describe a time in your life when you had to <u>face the music</u>.

Describe what you did that you had to face the music about and what happened.

_____

_____

_____

_____

_____

Exercise 68

Each sentence uses an idiom to describe a person. Finish each paragraph by giving a detail to support the first sentence.

 Start by working out what the idiom is telling you about the person.

1 Janet does not pull any punches. *She always tells you the truth even if it makes you feel bad.*

2 Tommy is getting too big for his boots. _____

3 Donnie is a bad egg. _____

4 Tamika is full of beans. _____

5 Zachary is a loose cannon. _____

6 Roland is a tough cookie. _____

Exercise 69

Each saying offers a lesson. Explain what the lesson is in your own words. Then give an example of a time you used, or could have used, the lesson.

1. Too many cooks spoil the broth.

    Lesson: _____

    _____

    Example: _____

    _____

    _____

    _____

2. The grass always looks greener on the other side.

    Lesson: _____

    _____

    Example: _____

    _____

    _____

    _____

Exercise 70

For each proverb, write a paragraph or two describing a situation in your life that showed that the saying is true.

 For the first question, you could describe a time where you got something because you were there first.

1   The early bird gets the worm.

_____

_____

_____

_____

2   You need to learn to walk before you can run.

_____

_____

_____

_____

Level 8

Exercises 71 to 80

Difficulty: ★★★

Building Your Vocabulary

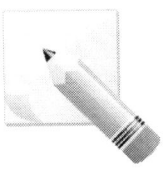

As you complete the exercises, list any words you have trouble with below. Draw a picture or write down the meaning of each word.

Exercise 71

Complete the idiom in each sentence with the correct color. Then explain the meaning of each sentence in your own words.

blue	red	black
gray	pink	green

1 The project was given the _____ light.

   _____

2 Desiree was feeling _____.

   _____

3 Samantha was tickled _____ by the present.

   _____

4 The broken vase made Tyra see _____.

   _____

5 The decision to be made is _____ and white.

   _____

6 Emi should use her _____ matter more often.

   _____

Exercise 72

Underline the idiom in each sentence. Then write the meaning of the idiom on the blank line.

1. I could not shake off the feeling that I had forgotten to do something.

   _____

2. I raced to the bus stop and was lucky to make it in the nick of time.

   _____

3. I was moved to tears by the way the novel ended.

   _____

4. My sisters fight a lot, and I always try to stay on the sidelines.

   _____

5. We racked our brains trying to think of something fun to do.

   _____

6. It was a close game, but the win slipped through our fingers.

   _____

Exercise 73

Complete each sentence.

 Start by thinking about what the idiom at the start of each sentence means. Then think of a way to finish the sentence that makes sense.

1 My heart sank when _____

   _____

2 Everything went down the drain because _____

   _____

3 The situation reached boiling point when _____

   _____

4 We were all walking on eggshells because _____

   _____

5 I got a slap on the wrist for _____

   _____

6 I had to go back to square one because _____

   _____

Exercise 74

List five situations where you might <u>keep your fingers crossed</u>.

1 _____

2 _____

3 _____

4 _____

5 _____

Choose one of the situations you listed above. Write a paragraph describing a time when you <u>kept your fingers crossed</u>. Explain what you kept your fingers crossed about and what happened in the end.

_____

_____

_____

_____

_____

_____

_____

Exercise 75

Complete each common simile. Use the pictures below as clues. Write the word that completes each simile on the blank line. Then use the simile in a sentence.

 Each simile can be used to describe what a person is like. Use this meaning of the simile in your sentence.

1 as tough as _____

_____

2 as sharp as a _____

_____

3 as fit as a _____

_____

4 as cool as a _____

_____

Exercise 76

Choose the best answer to each question.

1. Which sentence below includes an idiom?
   - Ⓐ Ivan and Lucas often fight about silly things.
   - Ⓑ They once fought over whether a bike was blue or green.
   - Ⓒ They usually manage to patch things up quite quickly.
   - Ⓓ They do sometimes get very angry with each other.

2. Which phrase means "to be unable to make any more progress"?
   - Ⓐ to hit a home run
   - Ⓑ to hit a nerve
   - Ⓒ to hit a brick wall
   - Ⓓ to hit a sour note

3. Which phrase means "to be very busy"?
   - Ⓐ to have the upper hand
   - Ⓑ to have your hands full
   - Ⓒ to have time on your hands
   - Ⓓ to have your hands tied

4. Which word completes the phrase that means "always together"?

   joined at the _____

   - Ⓐ heels
   - Ⓑ hip
   - Ⓒ feet
   - Ⓓ hands

5. What does the underlined word in the sentence below mean?

   By the end of the first chapter, I was <u>hooked</u>.

   - Ⓐ very bored
   - Ⓑ very confused
   - Ⓒ very relaxed
   - Ⓓ very interested

Exercise 77

Describe a time when you <u>bit off more than you could chew</u>.

> Remember that the underlined phrase is not actually referring to eating. Think about what special meaning the phrase has.

_____
_____
_____
_____
_____

Describe a time in your life when you <u>saw someone's true colors</u>.

> Describe what happened and what you learned about the person.

_____
_____
_____
_____
_____

Exercise 78

Write two or three lines of dialogue that include the given sentence.

1 You're telling me!

"This hill is too steep. I need to rest."
"You're telling me! I can't go any farther."

2 Knock it off.

3 Dream on!

4 You have got to be kidding!

Exercise 79

Each saying offers a lesson. Explain what the lesson is in your own words. Then give an example of a time you used, or could have used, the lesson.

1. A watched pot never boils.

    Lesson: _____

    _____

    Example: _____

    _____

    _____

    _____

2. Actions speak louder than words.

    Lesson: _____

    _____

    Example: _____

    _____

    _____

    _____

Exercise 80

Each proverb below gives advice. For each proverb, write a paragraph or two explaining whether you think it is good advice. Explain why you feel that way.

 If you think the proverb gives good advice, you could explain what people would gain by following the advice.

1   If something is worth doing, it's worth doing well.

_____

_____

_____

_____

_____

2   It's important to stop and smell the roses.

_____

_____

_____

_____

_____

Level 9

Exercises 81 to 90

Difficulty:

Building Your Vocabulary

As you complete the exercises, list any words you have trouble with below. Draw a picture or write down the meaning of each word.

Exercise 81

Complete each sentence with the idiom below that best fits. Then explain the meaning of each sentence in your own words.

to stick around	to bow out	to stop by
to clear up	to cut down on	to hold off

1 I tried _____ on making a decision.

   _____

2 I wanted _____ for a bit longer.

   _____

3 I chose _____ of the contest.

   _____

4 I had _____ a misunderstanding.

   _____

5 I decided _____ eating sweets.

   _____

6 I often like _____ the library.

   _____

Exercise 82

Underline the idiom in each sentence. Then write the meaning of the idiom on the blank line.

1. I tell Jenna to ignore her brother's teasing, but she <u>takes it to heart</u>.

   _____

2. I have been learning piano for months, and am only just <u>getting the hang of it</u>.

   _____

3. Before she left for Chile, Mary decided to <u>brush up</u> on her Spanish.

   _____

4. Etu was too busy, so he decided to <u>step down</u> from his role as class president.

   _____

5. I was annoyed that Greta was late, but I decided to <u>let it slide</u>.

   _____

6. The school had to <u>pull the plug</u> on the class trip because of the bad weather.

   _____

Exercise 83

Write the meaning of each idiom on the line. Then use the idiom in a sentence.

 Remember to use the special meaning of each phrase, and not the literal meaning.

1. put your feet up   *relax and unwind*

   It is nice to put your feet up at the end of the day.

2. put two and two together   _____

   _____

3. jump off the page   _____

   _____

4. hit a home run   _____

   _____

5. under lock and key   _____

   _____

6. hot under the collar   _____

   _____

Vocabulary Skills Workbook: Idioms, Adages, Similes, & Metaphors

Exercise 84

List five situations where someone might <u>tell a white lie</u>.

1 _____

2 _____

3 _____

4 _____

5 _____

Choose one of the situations you listed above. Write a paragraph describing a situation where someone <u>tells a white lie</u>. It could be real or made up. Describe the lie the person tells and why the person tells it.

_____

_____

_____

_____

_____

_____

Exercise 85

Each sentence below uses a metaphor. Explain the meaning of each sentence in your own words.

1. Fiona's room is a pigsty.

   _____

2. My memory of the trip is foggy.

   _____

3. The news was music to my ears.

   _____

4. My baby brother is the light of my life.

   _____

5. The basketball players are a well-oiled machine.

   _____

6. Frank has a roadmap to reach his goals.

   _____

Vocabulary Skills Workbook: Idioms, Adages, Similes, & Metaphors

Exercise 86

Choose the best answer to each question.

1. Which word could best replace *walked* to show that Mary is angry?

    Mary banged her hand on the table and then walked out.

    Ⓐ wandered Ⓒ trotted
    Ⓑ stormed   Ⓓ stepped

2. Which phrase means "to avoid being embarrassed"?
    Ⓐ to save face   Ⓒ to save money
    Ⓑ to save the day   Ⓓ to save your breath

3. A person described as "down-to-earth" is
    Ⓐ polite   Ⓒ sensible
    Ⓑ clumsy   Ⓓ grumpy

4. What does the underlined phrase in the sentence below mean?

    The deal to sell the company was done behind closed doors.

    Ⓐ quickly   Ⓑ secretly   Ⓒ carefully   Ⓓ calmly

5. Which word completes the phrase that means "to work something out"?

    join the _____

    Ⓐ club   Ⓑ dots   Ⓒ fray   Ⓓ team

Exercise 87

Describe a time when you had <u>a gut feeling about something.</u>

Describe what you had a gut feeling about and whether you were right.

_____

_____

_____

_____

_____

Describe a time in your life when someone <u>made a mountain out of a molehill</u>.

_____

_____

_____

_____

_____

_____

Exercise 88

Idioms and phrases can make stories more interesting or more exciting. Write a paragraph or two that includes any two of the phrases listed.

1 asking for trouble   rack my brains   nerves of steel

_____

_____

_____

_____

_____

2 neck and neck   against all odds   pick up the pace

_____

_____

_____

_____

_____

Exercise 89

Each saying offers a lesson. Explain what the lesson is in your own words. Then give an example of a time you used, or could have used, the lesson.

1   Pride comes before a fall.

   Lesson: _____

   _____

   Example: _____

   _____

   _____

   _____

2   All that glitters is not gold.

   Lesson: _____

   _____

   Example: _____

   _____

   _____

   _____

Exercise 90

For each proverb, write a paragraph or two describing a situation in your life that showed that the saying is true.

 For the first question, you could describe a time where someone wasted money, bought something silly, or was tricked into giving money away.

1   A fool and his money are soon parted.

_____

_____

_____

_____

_____

2   You shouldn't count your chickens before they hatch.

_____

_____

_____

_____

_____

Level 10

Exercises 91 to 101

Difficulty: ★★★

Building Your Vocabulary

As you complete the exercises, list any words you have trouble with below. Draw a picture or write down the meaning of each word.

Exercise 91

Complete the idiom in each sentence with the correct animal. Then explain the meaning of each sentence in your own words.

butterflies	fish	bull
flies	deer	crocodile

1 Denise looked like a _____ caught in the headlights.

   _____

2 Sergei was like a _____ in a china shop.

   _____

3 Winning the game was like shooting _____ in a barrel.

   _____

4 I knew that Luke was only crying _____ tears.

   _____

5 I had _____ in my stomach.

   _____

6 The skaters in the contest were dropping like _____.

   _____

Exercise 92

Underline the idiom in each sentence. Then write the meaning of the idiom on the blank line.

1. I looked high and low for my necklace, but I still could not find it.

   _____

2. I missed out on hearing most of the lesson because I was lost in thought.

   _____

3. I wasn't sure if my teammates would listen, but I put in my two cents anyway.

   _____

4. Helena would not lift a finger to help, which made her mother very upset.

   _____

5. Adam did not seem to be listening to me at all, so I decided to change tack.

   _____

6. The idea for the winning story I wrote came out of thin air.

   _____

Exercise 93

Complete each sentence.

 Start by thinking about what the idiom at the start of each sentence means. Then think of a way to finish the sentence that makes sense.

1 I was in a tight spot because _____

_____

2 Sean threw a spanner in the works when he _____

_____

3 I went out on a limb by _____

_____

4 Carina made waves when she _____

_____

5 People make my blood boil when they _____

_____

6 It feels like time flies when I am _____

_____

Exercise 94

List five things someone might <u>put on the back burner</u>.

1 _____

2 _____

3 _____

4 _____

5 _____

Choose one of the things you listed above. Write a paragraph describing a situation where someone <u>put something on the back burner</u>. Explain what the person put on the back burner and why they put it on the back burner.

_____

_____

_____

_____

_____

_____

Exercise 95

Complete each common simile. Use the pictures below as clues. Write the word that completes each simile on the blank line. Then use the simile in a sentence.

1 as clear as _____

_____

2 eyes like a _____

_____

3 as stubborn as a _____

_____

4 as smooth as _____

_____

Exercise 96

Choose the best answer to each question.

1. Which sentence below includes an exaggeration?
   - Ⓐ I knew it was going to be a long day at school.
   - Ⓑ I had to study math, science, and also music.
   - Ⓒ I put four textbooks and my lunch into my backpack.
   - Ⓓ My backpack would only just close and it weighed a ton.

2. Which phrase means "to be in a good position"?
   - Ⓐ sitting pretty
   - Ⓑ sitting tight
   - Ⓒ sitting on the fence
   - Ⓓ sitting on your hands

3. If people are described as "hanging on every word," what are they doing?
   - Ⓐ recording what is said
   - Ⓑ listening very closely
   - Ⓒ mistrusting what they hear
   - Ⓓ laughing at what someone is saying

4. Which reply to the sentence below would best show that you do not believe it will happen?

   "I am going to win an Academy Award one day."

   - Ⓐ Hold on.
   - Ⓑ March on.
   - Ⓒ Party on.
   - Ⓓ Dream on.

5. What does the underlined phrase in the sentence below mean?

   It took a lot of <u>elbow grease</u> to get the old bike cleaned up.

   - Ⓐ effort
   - Ⓑ patience
   - Ⓒ planning
   - Ⓓ tools

Exercise 97

Describe a time when you <u>had to bite your tongue</u>.

Describe what you bit your tongue about and why.

_____

_____

_____

_____

_____

Describe a time in your life when you <u>went against the grain</u>.

Describe what you did and why it went against the grain.

_____

_____

_____

_____

_____

Vocabulary Skills Workbook: Idioms, Adages, Similes, & Metaphors

Exercise 98

Idioms and phrases can make stories more interesting or more exciting. Write a paragraph or two that includes at least two of the phrases listed.

1   recipe for disaster   a sinking feeling   quaking in our boots

2   vanish into thin air   lost for words   in an instant

Exercise 99

Each saying offers a lesson. Explain what the lesson is in your own words. Then give an example of a time you used, or could have used, the lesson.

1 You can lead a horse to water, but you can't make it drink.

   Lesson: _____

   _____

   Example: _____

   _____

   _____

   _____

2 A chain is only as strong as its weakest link.

   Lesson: _____

   _____

   Example: _____

   _____

   _____

   _____

Exercise 100

A proverb is a common saying that states a truth. For each proverb, write a paragraph or two explaining whether or not you agree. Explain why you feel that way.

1   Two wrongs don't make a right.

_____

_____

_____

_____

_____

2   Fortune favors the brave.

_____

_____

_____

_____

_____

Exercise 101

Exaggeration can be used to make things sound more interesting or to make a point. Explain the meaning of each example of exaggeration.

1 We had to walk a million miles today.

   _____

2 My new shoes were killing my feet.

   _____

3 I could have slept for a whole century.

   _____

4 We had to wait forever for the bus.

   _____

5 You can hear Graham's snoring a mile away.

   _____

6 I could beat you at tennis standing on my head.

   _____

Hyperbole Challenge

Hyperbole is the use of exaggeration to describe something.

> Example: The class was so boring that all the students fell fast asleep within minutes.

It is not likely that all the students would have actually fallen asleep right away. However, this detail emphasizes how boring the class was.

Use hyperbole to complete each sentence below. Try to think of a detail that will emphasize the quality being described.

1 The food was so horrible that _____

_____

2 The rain was so heavy that _____

_____

3 The music was so loud that _____

_____

4 The chili was so spicy that _____

_____

5 The bedroom was so messy that _____

_____

6 The puppy was so cute that _____

_____

7 The building was so tall that _____

_____

8 The mall was so busy that _____

_____

9 I was so angry that _____

_____

10 The old house was so creepy that _____

_____

11 The movie star was so famous that _____

_____

12 My friend is so clever that _____

_____

Answer Key

Level 1: Exercises 1 to 10

Exercise 1
Explanations of sentence meaning may vary slightly. Sample meanings are given below.
1. books / It was time to study.
2. cake / The test was easy.
3. cup of tea / I did not like the music.
4. plate / I had a lot to do.
5. moon / I was happy about the win.

Exercise 2
The sentences and phrases should be matched as below.
I was hopping mad. → I was angry.
I was down in the dumps. → I was sad.
I was run off my feet. → I was busy.
I was shaking all over. → I was scared.
I was beat. → I was tired.
I was walking on air. → I was happy.
Button your lip. → Be quiet.
Get a move on. → Hurry up.
Hold your horses. → Wait.
Shoot for the stars. → Aim high.
Take it easy. → Calm down.

Exercise 3
1. stick around   2. a handful   3. got to run   4. slipped up   5. hit the hay   6. little by little

Exercise 4
Answers will vary. Any reasonable answer can be accepted.

Exercise 5
1. as big as an elephant   2. as slow as a snail   3. as free as a bird   4. as sick as a dog
5. as busy as a bee   6. as wise as an owl   7. as hungry as a bear   8. as quiet as a mouse

Exercise 6
1. C   2. C   3. D   4. C   5. B

Exercise 7
Answers will vary. Any reasonable answer can be accepted.

Exercise 8
1. lemon   2. green   3. cat   4. wool   5. wind   6. bag

Exercise 9
Answers will vary. Any reasonable explanation of the meaning of the saying is acceptable.

Exercise 10
1. trees   2. eggs   3. cake   4. worm   5. chickens   6. roses   7. apple   8. fire   9. grass   10. horse

Level 2: Exercises 11 to 20

Exercise 11
Sentences will vary. Any sentence that uses the idiom correctly can be accepted.
1. cloud   2. towel   3. hay   4. bell   5. beans

Exercise 12
The meaning given may vary slightly. Sample meanings are given below.
1. easily   2. sick   3. nearby   4. close   5. exactly
6. watch   7. quickly   8. understand   9. go faster   10. help me

Exercise 13
1. right away   2. cut it out   3. hit it off   4. get a move on   5. around the clock   6. by heart

Exercise 14
Answers will vary. Any reasonable answer can be accepted.

Exercise 15
1. as thin as a rake   2. as solid as a rock   3. as cold as ice   4. as light as a feather
5. as dry as a bone   6. as bright as the sun   7. as clear as a bell   8. as red as a tomato

Exercise 16
1. B   2. A   3. A   4. C   5. C

Exercise 17
Answers will vary. Any reasonable answer can be accepted.

Exercise 18
1. red-handed   2. duck   3. cat   4. fly   5. leaf   6. deep

Exercise 19
Answers will vary. Any reasonable explanation of the lesson of the saying and any reasonable example can be accepted.

Exercise 20
1. fire   2. forest   3. baby   4. cat   5. bird   6. dog   7. horse   8. glass   9. hay   10. leopard

Level 3: Exercises 21 to 30

Exercise 21
Sentences will vary. Any sentence that uses the idiom correctly can be accepted.
1. books   2. fence   3. page   4. light   5. boat

Exercise 22
The meaning given may vary slightly. Sample meanings are given below.
1. laughing a lot   2. very cheap   3. listening closely   4. took shortcuts   5. promised
6. very easy   7. from the start   8. very different   9. got tired   10. feeling scared

Exercise 23
1. like clockwork   2. in a flash   3. up and running   4. face to face   5. come in handy   6. on a roll

Exercise 24
Answers will vary. Any reasonable answer can be accepted.

Exercise 25
1. as brave as a lion   2. as sly as a fox   3. as proud as a peacock   4. as strong as a bull/as strong as an ox
5. as busy as a beaver   6. as gentle as lamb   7. as hungry as a wolf   8. as slippery as an eel

Exercise 26
1. C   2. B   3. D   4. C   5. A

Exercise 27
Answers will vary. Any reasonable answer can be accepted.

Exercise 28
1. dark   2. bush   3. hat   4. wire   5. knives   6. leg

Exercise 29
Answers will vary. Any reasonable explanation of the lesson of the saying and any reasonable example can be accepted.

Exercise 30
1. shy   2. burned   3. sorry   4. free   5. golden   6. right   7. never   8. hot   9. present   10. broken

Level 4: Exercises 31 to 40

Exercise 31
Sentences will vary. Any sentence that uses the idiom correctly can be accepted.
1. roll   2. sailing   3. heart   4. whale   5. blanket

Exercise 32
The meaning given may vary slightly. The words to be underlined and sample meanings are given below.
1. cost an arm and a leg / cost a lot of money
2. came clean about it / told the truth
3. right up my alley / something that interested me
4. a barrel of laughs / lots of fun
5. a shot in the dark / a guess
6. make head or tail of it / understand it

Exercise 33
1. steer clear of   2. gave a big hand   3. have a soft spot for
4. keep a straight face   5. out of the blue   6. for a song

Exercise 34
Answers will vary. Any reasonable answer can be accepted.

Exercise 35
Sentences will vary. Any sentence that uses the simile correctly can be accepted.
1. as pretty as a picture   2. as warm as toast   3. as easy as pie   4. as fresh as a daisy

Exercise 36
1. C   2. B   3. A   4. C   5. C

Exercise 37
Answers will vary. Any reasonable answer can be accepted.

Exercise 38
Answers will vary. Any detail or example given that supports the first sentence is acceptable.

Exercise 39
Answers will vary. Any reasonable explanation of the lesson of the saying and any reasonable example can be accepted.

Exercise 40
Answers will vary. Any reasonable explanation of why the student does or does not agree can be accepted. Students should give a personal opinion and provide an explanation to support the opinion.

Level 5: Exercises 41 to 50

Exercise 41
The meaning given may vary slightly. The words to be used and sample meanings are given below.
1. blue moon / It happens very rarely.
2. the bed / He got up in a bad mood.
3. eye to eye / They did not agree.
4. new leaf / She made a new start.
5. cats and dogs / It was raining heavily.
6. your court / It is up to you.

Exercise 42
The meaning given may vary slightly. The words to be underlined and sample meanings are given below.
1. in two minds / undecided
2. flies off the handle / gets very upset
3. not set in stone / could be changed
4. start from scratch / start all over again
5. sleep on it / think about it overnight
6. pull their weight / do their share of work

Exercise 43
Answers will vary. Any reasonable ending to the sentence that makes sense in context can be accepted.

Exercise 44
Answers will vary. Any reasonable answer can be accepted.

Exercise 45
Sentences will vary. Any sentence that uses the simile correctly can be accepted.
1. as tough as nails   2. sing like a bird   3. as white as a ghost   4. as fast as lightning

Exercise 46
1. D   2. C   3. B   4. D   5. A

Exercise 47
Answers will vary. Any reasonable answer can be accepted.

Exercise 48
Answers will vary. Any dialogue that includes the given sentence and uses it in a correct context can be accepted.

Exercise 49
Answers will vary. Any reasonable explanation of the lesson of the saying and any reasonable example can be accepted.

Exercise 50
Answers will vary. Any answer that refers to a time where the lesson of the proverb is relevant can be accepted. Students should use a personal experience to relate to the proverb and its meaning.

Level 6: Exercises 51 to 60

Exercise 51
The meaning given may vary slightly. The words to be used and sample meanings are given below.
1. the crack of dawn / We got up very early.
2. the bag / I let out the secret.
3. the kitchen sink / He packed almost everything.
4. the wrong tree / She was incorrect.
5. the same boat / We were all in the same situation.
6. the world / I felt very happy.

Exercise 52
The meaning given may vary slightly. The words to be underlined and sample meanings are given below.
1. having deep pockets / being rich
2. dragged her feet / delayed
3. on edge / nervous
4. on their toes / ready to act
5. on the same page / in agreement
6. bone to pick / problem to talk about

Exercise 53
The meaning given may vary slightly. Sample meanings are given below. Any sentence that uses the idiom correctly can be accepted.
1. had a good idea   2. quickly/at any time   3. yelled at me
4. correct/exactly right   5. close/about right   6. became angry

Exercise 54
Answers will vary. Any reasonable answer can be accepted.

Exercise 55
Sentences will vary. Any sentence that uses the simile correctly can be accepted.
1. sleep like a baby   2. as old as the hills   3. as good as gold   4. as straight as an arrow

Exercise 56
1. B   2. A   3. C   4. B   5. B

Exercise 57
Answers will vary. Any reasonable answer can be accepted.

Exercise 58
Answers will vary. Any paragraph that includes at least two of the phrases is acceptable.

Exercise 59
Answers will vary. Any reasonable explanation of the lesson of the saying and any reasonable example can be accepted.

Exercise 60
Answers will vary. Any reasonable explanation of why the student does or does not agree can be accepted. Students should give a personal opinion and provide an explanation to support the opinion.

Level 7: Exercises 61 to 70

Exercise 61
1. rat 2. whale 3. sheep 4. bear 5. hog 6. goat 7. bull 8. horses 9. ducks

Exercise 62
The meaning given may vary slightly. The words to be underlined and sample meanings are given below.
1. chewing the fat / chatting
2. kicking myself / upset with myself
3. out of the question / not at all possible
4. hit a snag / came across a problem
5. a bundle of nerves / very nervous
6. went out the window / was gone

Exercise 63
The meaning given may vary slightly. The words to be used and sample meanings are given below.
1. like wildfire / The news spread quickly.
2. on the blink / The fridge is broken.
3. iron out / We had to solve some problems.
4. a walk in the park / The test was easy.
5. hit the road / We left at eight o'clock.
6. had a blast / Everyone had a great time at the party.

Exercise 64
Answers will vary. Any reasonable answer can be accepted.

Exercise 65
The meaning given may vary slightly. Sample meanings are given below.
1. Chandra is very brave. 2. Sonny gets up early in the morning. 3. Natasha is being childish.
4. Felipe is very kind. 5. Patrick is always being silly. 6. Erica is the best player our softball team has.

Exercise 66
1. D   2. C   3. A   4. D   5. B

Exercise 67
Answers will vary. Any reasonable answer can be accepted.

Exercise 68
Answers will vary. Any detail or example given that supports the first sentence is acceptable.

Exercise 69
Answers will vary. Any reasonable explanation of the lesson of the saying and any reasonable example can be accepted.

Exercise 70
Answers will vary. Any answer that refers to a time where the lesson of the proverb is relevant can be accepted. Students should use a personal experience to relate to the proverb and its meaning.

Level 8: Exercises 71 to 80

Exercise 71
The meaning given may vary slightly. The words to be used and sample meanings are given below.
1. green / The project was allowed to go ahead.
2. blue / Desiree was feeling sad.
3. pink / Samantha was very happy with the present.
4. red / The broken vase made Tyra mad.
5. black / The decision to be made is clear.
6. gray / Emi should think more often.

Exercise 72
The meaning given may vary slightly. The words to be underlined and sample meanings are given below.
1. shake off / forget
2. in the nick of time / just in time
3. moved to tears / upset by
4. stay on the sidelines / not get involved
5. racked our brains / thought hard
6. slipped through our fingers / just got away

Exercise 73
Answers will vary. Any reasonable ending to the sentence that makes sense in context can be accepted.

Exercise 74
Answers will vary. Any reasonable answer can be accepted.

Exercise 75
Sentences will vary. Any sentence that uses the simile correctly can be accepted.
1. as tough as old boots   2. as sharp as a tack   3. as fit as a fiddle   4. as cool as a cucumber

Exercise 76
1. C   2. C   3. B   4. B   5. D

Exercise 77
Answers will vary. Any reasonable answer can be accepted.

Exercise 78
Answers will vary. Any dialogue that includes the given sentence and uses it in a correct context can be accepted.

Exercise 79
Answers will vary. Any reasonable explanation of the lesson of the saying and any reasonable example can be accepted.

Exercise 80
Answers will vary. Any reasonable explanation of why the student thinks the proverb does or does not give good advice can be accepted. Students should give a personal opinion and provide an explanation to support the opinion.

Level 9: Exercises 81 to 90

Exercise 81
The meaning given may vary slightly. The words to be used and sample meanings are given below.
1. to hold off / I tried to delay making a decision.
2. to stick around / I wanted to stay longer.
3. to bow out / I chose to pull out of the contest.
4. to clear up / I had to fix a misunderstanding.
5. to cut down on / I decided to eat fewer sweets.
6. to stop by / I often like to visit the library.

Exercise 82
The meaning given may vary slightly. The words to be underlined and sample meanings are below.
1. takes it to heart / gets upset about it
2. getting the hang of it / getting used to it
3. brush up on / improve on
4. to step down / to quit
5. let it slide / ignore it
6. pull the plug / cancel

Exercise 83
The meaning given may vary slightly. Sample meanings are given below. Any sentence that uses the idiom correctly can be accepted.
1. relax and unwind   2. work something out   3. stand out a lot
4. do very well   5. locked up   6. very angry

Exercise 84
Answers will vary. Any reasonable answer can be accepted.

Exercise 85
The meaning given may vary slightly. Sample meanings are given below.
1. Fiona's room is very messy.
2. I do not remember the trip very well.
3. I was glad to hear the news.
4. My baby brother is very important to me.
5. The basketball players play well together.
6. Frank has a plan to reach his goals.

Exercise 86
1. B   2. A   3. C   4. B   5. B

Exercise 87
Answers will vary. Any reasonable answer can be accepted.

Exercise 88
Answers will vary. Any paragraph that includes at least two of the phrases is acceptable.

Exercise 89
Answers will vary. Any reasonable explanation of the lesson of the saying and any reasonable example can be accepted.

Exercise 90
Answers will vary. Any answer that refers to a time where the lesson of the proverb is relevant can be accepted. Students should use a personal experience to relate to the proverb and its meaning.

Vocabulary Skills Workbook: Idioms, Adages, Similes, & Metaphors

Level 10: Exercises 91 to 101

Exercise 91
The meaning given may vary slightly. The animal to be used and sample meanings are given below.
1. deer / Denise looked stunned and frightened.   2. bull / Sergei was clumsy.
3. fish / Winning the game was too easy.   4. crocodile / I knew that Luck was faking tears.
5. butterflies / I felt nervous.   6. flies / The skaters competing were dropping out fast.

Exercise 92
The meaning given may vary slightly. The words to be underlined and sample meanings are below.
1. high and low / in a lot of places
2. lost in thought / thinking about other things
3. put in my two cents / gave my opinion
4. lift a finger / do anything at all
5. change tack / try something different
6. out of thin air / from nowhere

Exercise 93
Answers will vary. Any reasonable ending to the sentence that makes sense can be accepted.

Exercise 94
Answers will vary. Any reasonable answer can be accepted.

Exercise 95
Sentences will vary. Any sentence that uses the simile correctly can be accepted.
1. as clear as crystal   2. eyes like a hawk   3. as stubborn as a mule   4. as smooth as silk

Exercise 96
1. D   2. A   3. B   4. D   5. A

Exercise 97
Answers will vary. Any reasonable answer can be accepted.

Exercise 98
Answers will vary. Any paragraph that includes at least two of the phrases is acceptable.

Exercise 99
Answers will vary. Any reasonable explanation and any reasonable example can be accepted.

Exercise 100
Answers will vary. Any reasonable explanation of why the student does or does not agree can be accepted. Students should give a personal opinion and provide an explanation to support the opinion.

Exercise 101
The meaning given may vary slightly. Sample meanings are given below.
1. We had to walk a long way today.
2. My new shows were hurting me a lot.
3. I could have slept for a long time.
4. We had to wait a long time for the bus.
5. Graham snores loudly.
6. I could easily beat you at tennis.

Texas Standards Alignment

About the TEKS

The state standards for Texas are known as the Texas Essential Knowledge and Skills, or TEKS. These standards describe what students are expected to know. Student learning is based on these standards throughout the year, and the STAAR tests taken at the end of the year are designed to assess whether students have the skills described in the standards.

Skill Development

This book is designed to focus on key language skills and develop student understanding to meet and then exceed grade level expectations. As well as specifically covering idioms, adages, similes, and metaphors, it also develops related reading and writing skills. The table on the following page lists the TEKS skills that are covered in this book.

While the aim is mainly to develop and enhance language skills, the skills learned will also improve performance on the STAAR Reading test and the STAAR Writing test.

STAAR Reading Test Prep

The STAAR Reading test is taken by students in grades 3, 4, and 5. While students learn all the TEKS skills throughout the year, the STAAR tests only assess a specific set of skills. The skills covered in this book that are assessed on the STAAR Reading tests for grades 3, 4, and 5 are highlighted in bold.

While students do not take STAAR tests in grade 2, the grade 2 skills are the foundation for the skills that are learned in later grades.

STAAR Writing Test Prep

The STAAR Writing test is taken by students in grade 4. The test includes two composition sections. Each section includes a writing prompt and requires students to produce original writing. The language skills developed in this book will encourage stronger word choices, allow students to convey ideas more precisely, produce more engaging writing, and help students produce writing that demonstrates a more advanced level of vocabulary and writing skill. These improvements will increase the scores received for the compositions.

The STAAR Writing test also includes revision and editing sections, where students correct or improve writing. The stronger understanding of words and language developed by the exercises in this book will improve student performance on these sections.

TEKS Skill Coverage

Grade 2	Reading/Vocabulary Development
	• Use context to determine the relevant meaning of unfamiliar words or multiple-meaning words.
	Reading/Comprehension of Literary Text/Sensory Language
	• Recognize that some words and phrases have literal and non-literal meanings.
	Writing
	• Write literary texts to express their ideas and feelings.
	• Write brief compositions about topics of interest to the student.
Grade 3	Reading/Vocabulary Development
	• **Use context to determine the relevant meaning of unfamiliar words or distinguish among multiple meaning words and homographs.**
	• Identify and apply playful uses of language.
	Reading/Comprehension of Literary Text/Sensory Language
	• **Identify language that creates a graphic visual experience and appeals to the senses.**
	Writing
	• Write literary texts to express their ideas and feelings.
	• Write about important personal experiences.
	• Write persuasive texts to influence the attitudes or actions of a specific audience on specific issues.
Grade 4	Reading/Vocabulary Development
	• **Use the context of the sentence to determine the meaning of unfamiliar words or multiple meaning words.**
	• Identify the meaning of common idioms.
	Reading/Comprehension of Literary Text/Sensory Language
	• **Identify the author's use of similes and metaphors to produce imagery.**
	Writing
	• Write literary texts to express their ideas and feelings.
	• Write about important personal experiences.
	• Write persuasive texts to influence the attitudes or actions of a specific audience on specific issues.
Grade 5	Reading/Vocabulary Development
	• **Use context to determine or clarify the meaning of unfamiliar or multiple meaning words.**
	• Identify and explain the meaning of common idioms, adages, and other sayings.
	Reading/Comprehension of Literary Text/Sensory Language
	• **Evaluate the impact of sensory details, imagery, and figurative language in literary text.**
	Writing
	• Write literary texts to express their ideas and feelings.
	• Write a personal narrative that conveys thoughts and feelings about an experience.
	• Write persuasive texts to influence the attitudes or actions of a specific audience on specific issues.

Made in the USA
San Bernardino, CA
04 March 2019